LADYBUG FACTS

AND

FOLKLORE

A gardener & naturalist
guide to ladybugs and their lore

by **L. Patricia Kite**

limited edition

LPK Science
Newark, CA

This book is dedicated to Hannahleigh, for luck

LADYBUG FACTS
AND FOLKLORE

A gardener and naturalist's guide
to ladybugs and their lore

copyright (c) 2006 by
L. Patricia Kite

Cover photos by Ron West
   Convergent ladybug
   Ladybug larva
   Mealybug destroyer

LPK Science
Newark, CA
USA

TABLE OF CONTENTS

Chapter One: Ladybug Facts

Chapter Two: Ladybugs Close-Up

Chapter Three: Ladybug Tales

Chapter Four: Ladybug Lore

Chapter One: LADYBUG FACTS
SO MANY LADYBUGS

There are at least 4,500 known species, or types, of ladybugs. They live almost all over the world. Ladybugs belong to the beetle family Coccinellidae, which means "little sphere," or little round body.

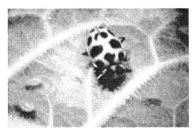

photo credit: InsectImages.org
R.J. Reynolds tobacco company slide set

In Great Britain there are about 42 ladybug species. There, the term "ladybird" is often used. This nickname goes back at least 600 years. At first only the 7 spotted lady beetle, or C-7, was called "ladybird." But after a while, many people called every lady beetle they saw a "ladybird."

In North America, there are about 400 ladybug species. In North America, most lady beetles are called "ladybugs." In this book, we'll use ladybugs. But you can call them what you please. See Chapter Three: "Ladybugs Have Many Names."

photos by Chris Schuster
www.chris-schuster.com/Licence

BUG VS. BEETLE?

What's the difference between a bug and a beetle? It's complicated, especially since most people call any insect a "bug." But beetles or *Coleoptera* have a pair of hard shiny forewings, or top wings. These are called elytra. The elytra in lady beetles and other beetles usually meet in a straight line down the back.

True bugs, or *Hemiptera*, often have front wings that

are divided in half.

photo credit: James L. Castner,
University of Florida Entomology Dept

In true bugs, the top wings are thick and leathery. Hind wings are slightly shorter than the front wings. The wings often do not meet in a straight line down the back, but have rounded or V-shapes.

What is another difference between a beetle and a true bug? Beetles, such as lady beetles, have chewing mouthparts. True bugs have long piercing mouthparts and suck up their food.

Beetle young do not look like their parents. Their appearance changes completely as they move from egg to larva to pupa to adult.

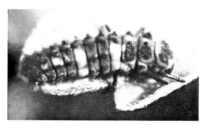

photo credit: Valerie

True bug young look almost like their parents except they don't have wings. True Bugs include squash bugs, stink bugs, assassin bugs, boxelder bugs, calico bugs, and squash bugs.

-4-

A LADYBUG RAINBOW

You may have seen reddish ladybugs. But there are also orange, dark brown, pink, gray, black and yellow ladybugs. Some ladybugs have spots. Some have none. There are ladybugs with as many as 24 spots. Spots can be red, white or black.

photo credit: Chris Schuster
www.chris-schuster.com/Licence

Some ladybugs have dashes or patterns instead of spots. And some ladybugs don't have any markings at all.

Ladybugs can be difficult to identify. Even within a single species, the number of spots can vary. In addition, spot placement can be different too. Even body color may vary within each species.

Many ladybugs are very tiny. Some are so tiny they are like the dot at the end of this sentence.

ARE YOU SURE IT'S A LADYBUG?

There's a ladybug mimic, also called a false ladybug. It looks pretty much like a ladybug. It is red and usually has five black spots, four on the body and one near the head. Actually it's another type of beetle, called the "handsome fungus beetle." It feeds on fungi. The handsome fungus beetle usually lives under decaying fungus-infested wood or by rotting fruit.

How can you tell the difference between a ladybug and a handsome fungus beetle? The latter has much longer antennae and is flatter in shape.

ARE YOU SURE IT'S A LADYBUG?

In the Philippines, there are small cockroaches resembling ladybugs. They are red or red-orange with black spots or black bands. The difference? Roaches have two very long antennae. Why the look-alike? Most predators avoid ladybugs as they have a terrible taste. Predators will eat cockroaches, but won't if they appear to be terrible-tasting ladybugs.

Chapter Two: <u>LADYBUGS CLOSE-UP</u>

A ladybug's hard shiny back is really made up of hardened forewings, or front wings. This is often called a "wing case." The scientific name is *elytron, or the plural elytra*. The elytra form a protective covering for a ladybug's delicate brown membranous wings. These delicate wings are kept folded underneath the hard wing case.

When the ladybug needs to fly, the wing cases separate along the back. The delicate wings underneath are now open for flight use. When a ladybug is flying, its wings may beat from 75 to 91 times per second.

Ladybugs don't see well. But on a ladybug's front are two antennae, or feelers. The antennae are a ladybug's sense of smell and touch. They also receive sound.

Like most beetles, most ladybugs have well developed chewing mouthparts or mandibles. Within the mouthparts are tiny teeth.

Ladybugs, like all insects, have 6 legs. Their six jointed legs are short, and are retractable, or can be pulled up, under the ladybug's body.

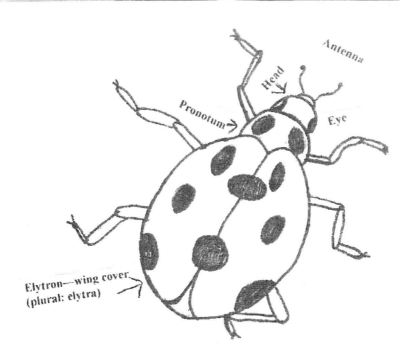

WHERE DO LADYBUGS LIVE?

Ladybugs live many different areas. Depending on type, they live in fields, farms, beaches, trees, shrubs and even houses. There's even a water ladybug. It is tan with black spots. The water ladybug lives in damp marshy places where it hides between reeds.

MILLIONS OF LADYBUGS

If it is a nice warm day when the new ladybugs emerge, they may fly in a swarm, or very large group. Helped by strong air currents, they can travel long distances. Sometimes millions of them are found on beaches, washed up by the sea. They are, perhaps, the weaker ladybugs, or those caught by waves. Or perhaps the wind has blown them off course.

The stronger ladybugs in a swarm have made their way to cities. They landed on roads and walls. Before people knew how helpful ladybugs were, people thought they were attacking. Fire engines were summoned to wash the ladybugs away.

Chapter Three : LADYBUG TALES
NAMING THE LADYBUG

A very common story goes back a long time in European history. It goes back to a time called the Middle Ages, between the 8th and the middle of the 15th century:

Many York farmers made their living growing hop vines. Hop vines have soft, cone-like, light green fruits. The fruits, when dried, were used to flavor different drinks [predominantly beer and medicinal]. However pest insects, such as aphids, feed on hop vines, as well as many other plants. This feeding can destroy plants.

In long-ago Europe, there came a time when there were a huge number of pest aphids. After a while, the farmers wondered if they would have any crop left. If all the hop vines died, the farmers couldn't earn a living. Perhaps they and their families would starve. The farmers prayed to the Virgin Mary, mother of Jesus, for help.

Suddenly in flew 1000s of little round red beetles with seven dark spots on their back. Three spots on each wing cover and one spot near the head. The beetles began eating all the pest insects. The crops were saved.

Many farmers believed the Virgin Mary, or Our Lady, had sent the rescuing little red insects from heaven. They began calling it "The Beetles of Our Lady." The Virgin Mary, in some old paintings, is shown wearing a red cloak. The seven ladybug spots represented her seven joys and seven sorrows. "The Beetles of Our Lady" slowly changed to "Lady Beetles."

LADYBUGS HAVE MANY NAMES

Ladybugs have at least 329 names from 55 countries. Of these, at least 80 names refer in some way to the Virgin Mary, and at least 50 names are dedicated to God. Historians believe that women thought of most ladybug names. In early times, women cared for animals that provided food, such as hens, chickens, calves, cows and lambs. You'll see these animals mentioned below in the ladybug name list. Men cared for the bigger animals, such as horses, bulls and oxen.

Here are just a few name samples from different countries:

North America: ladybugs, lady bugs, ladybirds, or lady beetles.

In England today they are most often called ladybird, but have also been called ladycow, ladyfly, lady-bee, Marygold, God's Little Cow, Bishop Barnaby, and Cushcow Lady.

Bosnia= buba mara

Iran= Ghasedak=Good News.

Norway=Goldsmith

Italy=Palomella=little dove, Porta Fortuna=luck bringer,

Vacchetta della Madonna, Coccinella, Lucia

China= Flower Lady

Poland= Biedronka, God's little cow

India=Indragopas=Indra's Cowherd, Sona Kida=golden insect

Holland= Lieveheersbeesjt=Dear Lord's animal

Ireland= Red soldier, God's cow

Israel=Parat Moshe Rabbenu = Cow of Moses our teacher

Germany=Marienkafer=Mary'sBeetles,

Sunnekuken=Sun's Little   Cow, Sonnerkafer=sun beetles.

Africa=Crop Picker

Iraq =Water Delivery-Man's Daughter.

Japan=Tentou Mushi [sun insect]

Sweden= Virgin Mary's golden hens, Keys of Heaven, Mary's maidservant's key, Nykelpiga , golden beetle

Scotland=ladyclocks

Greece= Paskalitsa

Korea=Mudangbule

Latvia= Mara or marite, after the long-ago Latvian goddess of earth power, Mara.

Czechoslavia: Slunecko=little sun

France= les betes du bon Dieu = creatures of the good God, Vaches de Dieu=cows of the Virgin, Coccinelle

Russia=Bozhia Korovka=God's Cow

Spain=Vaquilla de Dios=God's little cow, Arca de Dios=God's Ark, Mariquita

Malaysia: Kumbang

Egypt= um ali, um hassn [um= "mother"- every district has a name]

*Norway=*Mary's Hen

*Ethiopia=*Timziza

New Zealand Maori: Wahine Manu=ladybird

Austria= Gluckskafer

Native American Indian Cheyenne: Playing Card Beetle

*Portugal=*Joaninha, insect of love, good news

Iran: Fatemeh's bird, Good news, small spotted watermelon

Jordan= Da'asouqah, also sometimes called a "Volkswagen" due to ladybug shape

THE SCARAB

Some authors mention possibly tracing ladybug history to the Egyptian scarab beetle. The scarab beetle was the symbol of life in ancient Egypt. Scarab jewelry and scarab decorations were widely used. They have been found wherever the Egyptian traders traveled. Archaeologists, people who study ancient cultures, have discovered scarabs dating back before 3500 B.C. Scarab jewelry is still widely sold today as an Egyptian souvenir.

However the true scarab beetle is the dung beetle. Its scientific name is *Scarabaeus sacer*, which means "a sacred beetle." The male scarab beetle rolls balls of dung, or animal waste matter, into a ball. The female scarab beetle places an egg in each rolled dung ball. The ball will rest in a quiet spot until the egg hatches from it.

However people only saw the male beetle doing its dung rolling. They didn't know there was a female scarab beetle too. All scarabs were believed to be male.

Later, when a baby beetle emerged, ancient Egyptians thought this was the original male beetle, coming to life again fully formed. The beetle was supposed to have, within itself, the secret of eternal life. It was reborn, just like the soul of a man would be born again.

Just as the scarab beetle pushes its dung ball across the earth, ancient Egyptians believed Khepri, the scarab god, rolled the sun's ball across the sky. In this myth, Khepri pushes the sun into the Other World in the evening. In the morning, Khepri pushes the sun back into the sky. Just as the sun rolled across the heaven, reborn each day, so the scarab beetle signified life's renewal and a person's ability to exist Forever.

甲虫飛翔編

シークレット

How did the ladybug get into this picture? The ladybug got into the picture because it is often red or red-orange, like the sun. But, aside from being a beetle, it doesn't seem to have much relation to the Egyptian scarab beetle of myth.

photo credit: Valerie

THE JAGUAR

There is a reference in Exell that the ladybug, in Cherokee Native American mythological heritage, was connected with the jaguar, a large leopardlike mammal. Both are carnivorous, or meat eaters. Both have black spots, the jaguar on gold, and the 15-spotted ladybug on orange. In Cherokee heritage, a common name for the ladybug was called "A WEH SA," or creature living in water, a connection with the water-loving jaguar. However since this was such an important insect, A WEH Sa wouldn't be used in its presence. Instead it was called "A GIGA U E," translating as "Great Beloved Woman."

The Great Beloved Woman was the highest title a female could obtain in the Cherokee long-ago traditional society. One of her jobs was determining the fate of prisoners. When doing this, her face was painted orange-yellow, then painted with 15 dots.

CHAPTER FOUR: LADYBUG LORE
LADYBUG RHYMES

Girls or young women recited most ladybug rhymes. The rhymes usually wished for something: food, clothing, good weather, boyfriends, future husbands, knowing the number of children, and general luck. Of the many wished-for food items, butter, bread, cheese and honey lead the list. These have been food items for 100s of years, and some of the rhymes are quite old.

NORTH AMERICA

Ladybug, ladybug

Fly away home

Your house is on fire

Your children will burn.

GREAT BRITAIN

Cow-lady, cow-lady

Fly away home

Your house is all burnt,

And your children are gone.

GREAT BRITAIN:

Ladybug, ladybug

Fly away home!

    Your house is on fire,

Your children all gone

All but one, and her name is Ann,

And she crept under the pudding pan.

YORKSHIRE

Cusha-coo-lady, fly away home

Thy house is a-fire and all they bairns gone.

GREAT BRITAIN:

Ladybug, ladybug

Fly away home

Your house is on fire

Your children will burn

Except little Nan, who sits in a pan,

Weaving gold laces as fast as she can

GREAT BRITAIN

Ladybird, ladybird

Fly away home

Your house is on fire,

Your children are alone.

GREAT BRITAIN:

Lady-cow, lady-cow, fly away, flee!

Tell me which way my wedding's to be

Uphill, or downhill, or towards the brown Clee!

Bishop, Bishop Barnabee

Tell me when my wedding be;

If it be tomorrow day,

Take your wings and fly away!

Fly to the east, fly to the west,

Fly to him that I love the best.

GREAT BRITAIN:

Lady-cow, lady-cow, fly away, flee!

Tell me which way my wedding's to be

Uphill, or downhill, or towards the brown Clee!

GREAT BRITAIN:

Lady-bug, lady-bug, fly away home

Your house is on fire and your children alone

All burned but one,

And that's Brown Betty that sits in the sun

ITALY

Lucia, Lucia

Metti l'ali e vola via

FRANCE

Small manivole, fly, fly, fly!

Your father is at the schoolhouse, fly, fly, fly

He has brought you a beautiful gown, fly, fly, fly

If you don't fly, you will not have it.

FRANCE

Fly to the blue sky

Your nest is on fire

The Turks with their sword

Are going to kill your young

Hanneton, fly, fly. Hanneton, fly.

POLAND

Biedronka

Go to heaven and bring me

A piece of bread [blessings]

RUSSIA
Little cow of God,

Fly to the sky

God will give you bread

CHINA
Lady-bug, lady-bug

Fly away, do

Fly to the mountain

And feed upon dew

PHILLIPINES [song]
Ladybug, ladybug

How do you do?

How do you do?

Fly away, fly.

Golden Hen, golden hen, fly, fly

Let the weather tomorrow be full

Golden hen, golden hen, fly fly

They house is burning, thy children are gone

Little birdie, birdie

Fly to Marybrunn

And bring us a fine sun

Maerspart, fly the heaven

Bring me a sack full of biscuits,

One for me, one for thee

For all the little angels one

May-cat, fly away, hasten away

Bring me good weather with you tomorrow

GERMANY

Goldchaber, fly off, into the high spruce

To eat with Mother Anne

So, get your cheese and bread

It's better than the bitter death

GERMANY

Goldchaber, fly away.

Your house is burning

All your children

Are crying together

Tidbit: In Germany, songs about ladybugs were set to music by famous composers such as Johannes Brahms and Robert Schumann.

AUSTRALIA

Ladybird, ladybird

Fly away home!

Your house is on fire,

And your children all gone

All but one whose name is Ann,

Who hid herself under the frying pan.

LUCKY LADYBUGS?

Just about everybody likes ladybugs. They're supposed to bring good luck. The redder the insect, the better the luck. There are long-time ladybug superstitions almost all over the world.

According to a Norse legend, the ladybug came to earth riding on a bolt of lightening

Germany: ladybugs are the ones who bring babies to a home, a companion to stork and swan baby-bringer folklore. Also, ladybugs are believed so lucky, that ladybug ornaments are used for Christmas tree decorations.

India: it is bad luck to kill a ladybug. The souls of the dead are supposed to rest with this pretty insect.

In parts of Asia, people believed the ladybug understood what a person said.

Canada: if you find a ladybug in your house during the winter, you will receive as much money as it has spots on its back.   If you find a ladybug in your garage, you will have good luck.

Italy: When a child loses a tooth, the tooth is hidden in a little hole. A gift is expected from the ladybug,   Santu Nicola, in exchange for the tooth. When the child returns, there is a coin in the hole and the tooth is gone.

England: Hold a ladybug on your hand. Tell it to "fly away."   Whatever direction it flies is the   direction a boyfriend will come from. To farmers, a ladybug's presence predicts a good harvest.

Norway, if a man and woman spot a ladybug at the same time, they'll have a romance.

In parts of the United States, if a ladybug landed on your clothes, you would get another garment of the same type.

Belgium, people believed that if a ladybug crawled across the hand of a young girl, she would be married within a year. And if a ladybug landed on you, you should count its spots. That's the number of children you will have.

France, if a ladybug landed on you, then flew away, whatever illness you had would fly away with the ladybug. In the vineyards, a ladybug's presence signifies good weather.

Sweden, if a ladybug lands on you, then flies away, you will get a new dress with many spots.

Bosnia, when a ladybug lands on you, let it fly away on its own. The way it goes is the direction extra money comes from.

LADYBUG SUPERSTITIONS

Some people think that ladybugs can tell you the time of day, tell you how long you will live, or fly in the direction of lost cattle to help you locate them.

If a ladybug lands on your hand, you will get new gloves. If it lands on your dress, you will get a new dress.

If a ladybug creeps about a young lady's hands, it is measuring her for wedding gloves. The lady must watch which way the ladybug flies, for her sweetheart will arrive from that direction.

If a ladybug lands on you, don't brush it off. It's lucky. Let it fly away on its own.

If a ladybug lands on your hand, and crawls on each finger, that's very lucky.

If you count the spots on a ladybug that lands on you, each spot represents a happy month in your future

If you injure a ladybug, it will rain.

Harm a ladybug, and the Virgin will punish you for 9 days.

If you are sick and a ladybug lands on you, when it flies away it will take the sickness with it.

Put a ladybug on your hand and make a wish. When it flies away, that's the direction luck will come from.

A seven-spotted ladybug was thought to be a fairy's pet. If you see one, you can make three wishes.

If, by mistake, you kill a ladybug, you must bury its body, then stamp on the ground three times.

TIDBIT

The ladybug is a state insect of Delaware (1975), Iowa, Massachusetts (1974), New Hampshire (1977), New York (1989), Ohio (1975), and Tennessee (1975).

Chapter Five: LADYBUG LIFESTYLE
WHAT DO LADYBUGS EAT?

Most ladybugs eat pest insects. Scientists have counted how many aphids a single ladybug will eat in 2 ½ months. In one test count, a ladybug ate 7315 aphids! That's about 100 aphids per day. Another study said ladybugs eat about 50 aphids per hour! Female ladybugs seem to eat more aphids than male ladybugs.

Most ladybugs prefer aphids and scale insects as food. However there are exceptions. The 16 spot ladybug, 22 spot ladybug and the orange ladybug prefer meals of powdery mildew.

A few ladybugs feed only on a fungus that grows on plant leaves. The 24 spot ladybug only eats leaves of plants such as clover and chickweed. The Neoharmonia venusta ladybug prefers beetle larvae to aphids. Look for this ladybug on willow trees infested with Willow Leaf Beetles. There are also very tiny ladybugs that only dine on certain mites.

Some ladybugs prefer whitefly meals. Twice-stabbed ladybugs, common on tree trunks and branches, feed on scale and other soft, slow moving prey. The red and black Vedalia beetle is famous for its tremendous appetite for cottony-cushion scale.

When their normal food is scarce, aphid-eating ladybug adults and young will feed on flower nectar and honeydew. Honeydew is the sugary waste matter excreted, or given off, from aphids and whiteflies. Really hungry ladybugs will also feed on plant sap.

Sometimes people claim a ladybug has bitten them. It occasionally does happen! A starving ladybug may taste a person. Their nip feels like a pinprick. It may sting. The ladybug has, in nipping, given off a tiny drop of its digestive enzyme, a body chemical. That causes the stinging feeling. However people aren't the least tasty to a ladybug. After tasting, the ladybug departs very quickly.

LADYBUG MATING TIME

In spring, male and female ladybugs come out of their hibernation, or rest period. First they find food. Then mating begins. It is difficult to tell the difference between a male and female ladybug. In general, males are usually slightly smaller than females.

Mating tends to be a matter of chance. Males often find a mate by just bumping into her. Sometimes a male ladybug is attracted to a female of another ladybug species. She usually rejects him. Male ladybugs also may spend up to four hours mating with a dead female before realizing something is wrong.

Although aphid-eating ladybugs can survive on plant a mate. pollen, nectar and honeydew, most females must have aphid food in order to lay eggs. After mating, well-fed females soon begin placing light yellow or dark orange eggs on leaves, plant stems, or tree trunks. There may be 12 to 30 eggs in each clump, depending on species. A female ladybug will lay about 400 eggs in her one-year life span. Just as ladybugs have protective chemicals in their body, so do the eggs. They are not tasty to predators.

LADYBUG YOUNG

Ladybug babies come out of the eggs in one to six weeks, depending on species. They don't look anything like their parents. The babies, or larvae, have big heads, short legs, and no wings. They may have bright white, yellow, or orange spots plus body stripes. Less than ½ inch long, they are covered with bumps or spines. Their jaws are sickle-shaped. Some people think they look like tiny spiny alligators. The larvae eat pest aphids too. They eat as many

as they can.   photo: valerie

A hungry larva grows quickly. Its top skin is not stretchable. So, as each larva grows, its top skin becomes tighter. At three to seven day intervals, its top skin begins splitting. A larger ladybug larva crawls out of the top skin. Its old skin drops off.

Underneath the old skin is a new skin. The period between each skin shedding is scientifically called an "instar." The ladybug larva keeps on eating and growing.

Each larva may eat 350 pest aphids before changing into an adult. How do they feed? The larvae bite a hole in an aphid's body, and then suck out body liquids. As the larvae get bigger, they eat aphid legs and antennae too. The more larvae present, the fewer pest aphids remain to do damage.

Does an aphid ever try to escape? It may move to the side so the ladybug doesn't bump into it. If grabbed by the ladybug, it may kick. Or it may try to escape by dropping off the plant.

NASA TIDBIT In 1999, the National Aeronautics and Space Administration [NASA] sent four ladybugs into space. Aphids traveled with them. Why? It was an experiment. Aphids may try to escape ladybug capture by dropping off a plant. The Space Shuttle had zero gravity. Could the aphids escape from the ladybugs without being able to drop off using gravity? It seems not. Space shuttle ladybugs, working in zero gravity, caught and ate aphids. The people in the space shuttle named the ladybugs after the Beatles: John, Paul, Ringo and George.

MEDICAL TIDBIT: Ladybugs as medicine: Long ago, among other insects, ground up ladybugs were used as tooth powder and to get rid of toothaches. They were also prescribed as a remedy, or cure, for measles and infant colic.

FROM YOUNG TO ADULT

Ladybug skin shedding happens three times. In about a month, the larva is full size. Then, for a short time, it stops eating. Each ladybug larva attaches itself to the underside of a leaf by its tail end. It hangs there upside down. Now it contracts, or becomes shorter.

photo credit: Valerie

The skin of each larva splits open just once more. Underneath is a new shape. This is called a pupa. At first the pupa is soft and whitish. But it soon may turn orange, black brown, grey or white. It becomes dry, and hard. It appears somewhat humped over. Inside each pupa, an adult ladybug is forming.

About one week later, the skin of the pupa splits open. Hungry young adult ladybugs climb out of each pupa. Usually this happens in June, but may occur as late as August. It depends on the weather and ladybug species.

At first the new ladybugs rest. They open their elytra, or wing shields, and begin drying their wings. When hatching, they are a light color, but this soon darkens to their regular color. Feeding begins quickly.

While all this is happening, the parent generation begins dying. They have survived the winter, and provided eggs for new ladybugs. A ladybug's life span is about one year.

HOW DO LADYBUGS PROTECT THEMSELVES?

How do tiny ladybugs and their larvae protect themselves from enemies such as larger insects, birds and animals? First, their shiny hard outer wing covers are a protection. When attacked, ladybugs pull their six legs under their hard protective wing covers. At the same time, most can give off a yellowish fluid. This has a very bitter taste, and is a quite important protection. Their young and eggs also have this bitter tasting protection.

The bitter, bad smelling, yellow body fluid oozes out of the ladybug's leg joints. What is it? The scientific name is "reflex bleeding." The blood of most ladybugs not only stinks, but also often has alkaloids, or chemicals, in it that can make a hungry predator, or enemy, quite ill. After a predator nibbles on this bitter tasting, smelly, insect, they tend to leave all ladybugs alone in the future.

How do predators know it's a ladybug? Most ladybugs are brightly colored with spots or markings. Birds, especially, try to avoid eating anything with that warning coloration. However birds that fly very quickly, as swallows and swifts, get to the ladybugs so fast that the ladybug doesn't have time to give off its unpleasant fluid. So they may not pay attention to the warning colors.

Ladybugs may fall off a plant to escape. They also may "play dead" when in danger. Many predators won't eat an insect that doesn't move.

TIDBIT: Ladybugs that don't have bitter body fluids tend to be rather plain, and stay hidden.

PEOPLE as ENEMIES: People destroy enormous numbers of ladybugs. Chemicals used on plants kill ladybugs. Cars and trucks run over ladybugs. Ladybug winter shelter sites are bulldozed for housing and factories. People have gardens with few plants, so ladybugs can't find food. And, of course, the large-scale collection of ladybugs for sale to the gardener is causing, some believe, a long-term drop in ladybird populations.

LADYBUGS IN WINTER

Low temperatures make ladybugs inactive. Even if winter weather occasionally warms up, the lack of prey, as aphids, doesn't start ladybugs moving about a lot.

Ladybugs begin hiding in groups. They hide in sheltered spots and soon go to sleep. Their bodies survive on the fat stored from their spring and summer feeding. Groups vary in size, from about 24 ladybugs to several thousand.

Ladybugs can hibernate in snow. They can produce, inside their bodies, a form of ladybug anti-freeze that prevents ice crystals from forming within their bodies. But the winter mortality, or death rate, for ladybugs, is very high. They die from cold and disease.

Chapter Six: BIOLOGICAL CONTROL
THE CONVERGENT LADYBUG

In the United States there is a native reddish-orange ladybug. It usually has 6 black spots on each wing cover. It is called the Convergent ladybug or 12-spot ladybug.

In early summer, Convergent ladybugs usually fly away from hot dry farms, fields and gardens. They fly upward until they are about a mile high into the air. Here seasonal winds carry them into cooler Sierra Nevada mountain areas. Millions of ladybugs make this journey. In spring, when the weather warms up, ladybugs come out from their hidden places. Convergent ladybugs now fly back to fields, gardens, mountain meadows and farms.

convergent ladybug eating aphids

LADYBUGS: THE FIRST BIG BIOLOGICAL CONTROL

In the 1860s and 1870s, many Southern California citrus farmers grew orange and lemon trees. They relied on crop sales to make a living and take care of their families.

Then, in 1868, a new insect pest was accidentally introduced to California on imported Australian acacia trees. It was called "cottony cushion scale." Scale insects are very tiny insects usually hidden under a soft or hard covering. Cottony cushion scales have a fluffy cotton-like cover. Scales feed by sucking out plant juices. Scale feeding can kill plants.

These scale insects multiplied very quickly. By 1885 their feeding began destroying 1000s of orange and lemon trees. Insect-killing treatments with chemicals didn't work. In a short time, this destructive scale insect had spread to every orchard and orange tree in California.

The citrus farmers felt so helpless. They began burning their trees. They began to leave their ruined orchards. The farmers wondered if all their orange and lemon citrus trees would soon be gone. What would they do then?

Charles Valentine Riley, London born, had come to America in the 1860s. He worked as a laborer on a livestock farm in Kankakee, Illinois, and a co-publisher of a Chicago farming magazine. Eventually his growing expertise earned him an appointment to a new entomologist position in Missouri.

This began Riley's government work. In 1877, he became chief of the U.S. Entomological Commission. Later he served two terms as chief entomologist, or insect specialist, with the U.S. Department of Agriculture [USDA]. His reputation spread as a pioneer of biological Control: the use of one natural organism to control another.

Riley knew that cottony cushion scale didn't bother citrus trees in its home country. Why not? Did it have an enemy there? This called for some detective work, a different kind than before.

In 1887, Mr. Riley decided to send his assistant, entomologist Albert Koebele, to Australia to search for clues. However USDA employees were not allowed to travel overseas. So where would the travel money come from? C.V. Riley and others worked up a special project.

Instead of being from the USDA, Albert was sent to Australia by the U.S. State Department. Officially, he was representing America at an agricultural exposition in Melbourne, Australia.

Upon arrival, Albert Koebele began his search for cottony cushion scale enemies. He quickly discovered that a tiny red and black Australian lady beetle, called the Vedalia beetle, just loved to eat scale insects. He predicted that it would become famous in the United States.

Albert collected a few hundred Vedalia ladybugs, putting them in small containers. He sent them home by ship. Only 29 survived.

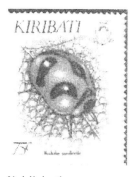

Vedalia beetle

Riley sent another batch, and then another, 514 altogether. D.W. Coquillet, an experienced amateur entomologist, had been selected to raise them. He did so in a mesh tents under scale-infested citrus trees. The ladybugs multiplied. Then they were released in Los Angeles at several orange and lemon tree groves.

Presto! Lady bugs began eating the scale. They ate and ate. They multiplied. The orange trees began to look healthier. Within two years, the scourge of cottony cushion scale was no more. Ladybugs had again come to the rescue! Gardeners and farmers carrying little boxes traveled from all over. They gathered ladybugs to take home with them.

Instead of using insecticides, which kill good insects as well as pests, a natural help had been found. This was the first time, in America, that beneficial insects had been used on a large scale to help the gardener and farmer. The total cost of the import was $1,500. To date, many millions of dollars have been saved. Today scientists research many different insects for use in "good" against "bad" bugs. It is part of what is now called "Biological Control."

MEALYBUG DESTROYER
ANOTHER BIOLOGICAL CONTROL

In 1891, Albert Koebele, the biological control pioneer that brought in the Vedalia ladybug, imported another ladybug. The Mealybug Destroyer came from Australia. Koebele brought it into California to control the citrus mealybug that was harming the citrus industry: lemons, oranges, and grapefruit.

What are mealybugs? Mealybugs are only ¼ inch long, but they do a lot of damage. Each mealybug is covered with white protecting waxy threads. When grouped together, they look like a batch of cotton fluff.

Mealybugs feed by sticking their straw-like hollow stylets into plants. The stylets suck up plant fluids. The loss of the nutritious fluids causes a plant to turn yellow and maybe die. On fruit trees, mealybug feeding also causes fruit drop and oddly colored fruit.

The Mealybug Destroyer ladybug adult is small, dark brown, and has a tan-orange head. However its young resemble pest mealybugs and are often destroyed by mistake. The Mealybug Destroyer ladybug and young eat many pest mealybugs. It is another biological control that helps reduce harmful pesticide use.

[ladybug] mealybug destroyer attacking mealybug pests

design your own ladybug

THE LADYBUG COLLECTORS

You may find the red ladybug with 12 black spots, *Hippodamia convergens,* for sale at garden centers or in garden catalogues. They are usually contained in a little plastic, mesh, or cardboard container. People called gatherers, pickers or collectors have gathered these ladybugs. Biocontrol, or the use of insects to control other insects, is now big business.

While this ladybug species is found wild everywhere in the United States, the only place where it gathers in large groups is in mountain areas. A major gathering area is in the mountains near Sacramento, California.

Most collectors vacuum up the ladybug masses. The collected ladybugs go into large cloth sacks. After collection, ladybugs are separated from any surrounding leaves or dirt. At first they are placed in big containers or tubs. From here they are scooped out into small or large containers. A large gallon container might have 75,000 ladybugs in it.

After packing, the ladybug containers go into coolers. Cooling slows their need to eat right away. Larger containers may be sent off to farmers. Or the containers may be sent to distributors who put them in the small packets seen at garden centers.

Hopefully the packaged ladybugs are released quickly. The ladybugs have done without food all winter. They must eat or they will starve, even within the containers. There is also no guarantee that the collected ladybugs are healthy. According to references, some, or many, may have fatal parasites.

When captured ladybugs are released into gardens and fields, they look for food right away. Otherwise the ladybugs fly away to where there is more food. There are several scientific studies looking for ways to get ladybugs to stay where they are released.

Chapter Seven: Pest Ladybugs

Are all ladybug species helpful? Not all. A very few are pests. Which ones?   The Mexican bean beetle, the bean leaf beetle and the squash beetle are pest ladybug relatives.

The Mexican bean beetle has 16 spots. It is coppery - yellow colored. Otherwise it resembles the helpful 12-spot orange-red ladybug. The Mexican bean beetle chews on the leaves, pods and stems of green, lima and soybeans.

Bean leaf beetles are another pest relative of the good ladybug beetle. They are pale yellow to dull red with three or four black spots, and a triangle spot near the head. They chew on the leaves of peas, beans, cowpeas and soybeans. Bean leaf beetle feeding makes plant leaves look like lace.

Squash beetles feed on squash, pumpkins and melon leaves. These common beetles are yellow with seven black spots on each wing cover. All three of these pest beetles can stay in your garden or farm all year. In winter, they tend to hide under plant waste.

HARLEQUIN LADY BEETLE

There is also a ladybug that is both helpful and a pest. It is called the "Multicolored Asian Lady Beetle." This ladybug is also called "Halloween Lady Beetle," Japanese lady beetle, and Harlequin lady beetle.

The Harlequin ladybug is one of the larger ladybugs. It is about ¼ inch long. It comes in many different colors. A Harlequin beetle may be yellow, pumpkin orange, black or red. Harlequin means multi-colored. These beetles may have zero spots or up to 20 black or faded spots. Most have a white area just behind the head with a black M-shaped marking on it. Harlequin ladybugs are often confused with other, more beneficial, ladybugs.

photo credit: Valerie

Scientists are still discussing how the multicolored ladybug got so plentiful in North America. Some say by accident. Others mention that 1000s of these beetles were brought in about 20 years ago by the U.S. Department of Agriculture [USDA] in an attempt to control tree-feeding aphids and scale insects.

In Asia, this pretty ladybug ate aphids and other small soft insects that lived in trees. In winter, they hibernated in the cracks of cliffs. However many parts of North America and Europe lack cliffs. However buildings seem to appear like cliffs to the Harlequin ladybug. So they mass on buildings. They wander into houses, garages, attics and basements looking for a comfortable winter's napping site.

Seeking shelter in a house area is a main difference between the Harlequin ladybug and other ladybugs. Most ladybugs hibernate, or winter sleep, in sheltered sites outdoors.

The multicolored or harlequin ladybug is causing another problem in some areas. They have such a big appetite for pest insects, they don't leave much for native ladybugs. So in some areas, these starve. Also, if food gets really scarce, the Harlequin ladybug will eat other ladybugs. So the entire ladybug population in an area gets smaller.

What to do? Scientists are working on the problem. While this imported ladybug can be a nuisance at times, like most other ladybugs, the Harlequin ladybug eats a lot of pest insects.

Chapter Eight:
ATTRACTING AND KEEPING LADYBUGS

Imported ladybugs seldom stay where you put them. If they land in your garden and there's no food, they fly away quickly. If they don't find food before they use up the rest of their winter fat reserves, or storage, they will die of starvation. This period may be as short as two days.

If you want the best results from ladybug appetites, try to attract native ladybugs instead of those purchased from far-away areas. Grow plants that attract them. Flowers attracting ladybugs include dill, hibiscus, passionflower, morning glory, impatiens, and angelica. Trees attracting ladybugs include flowering cherry, nectarine, peach, plum, almond, chokecherry, plus the fruit trees plum, peach, cherry, nectarine, apricot, prune and almond.

Do not use pesticides. Pesticides include herbicides, fungicides and insecticides. Whatever will kill pest insects will kill ladybugs too.

If you buy imported ladybugs, these ideas may help: Use a protective mulch around plants to give ladybugs a place to hide. Water down the garden area. Then release purchased ladybugs in the early evening. When it is cool outside, ladybugs aren't as active. Place them gently at the base of aphid-infested plants.

How many ladybugs will you need to purchase? One-half pint, about 4,500 ladybugs, should be enough for a garden 50 x 60 feet. Again, if you buy purchased ladybugs that have been kept in a garden nursery outdoor container of any kind, remember that if they haven't eaten in a few days, they are not healthy and may be dying within the container.

There must be many aphids in the garden if you want your purchased ladybugs to stay around. If you have purchased a ½ pint container of ladybugs, there must be at least 200,000 ladybugs available for an instant meal. If not, the ladybugs will leave promptly.

In one springtime test, researchers released 400,000 marked ladybugs in a known area. Within three weeks, not one ladybug could be found where they were released. Researchers kept looking for them. They finally found 19 of the specially marked ladybugs. They were seven miles away from the original release area!

LADYBUGS AS PETS?

Ladybugs must eat. Most ladybugs eat aphids and other tiny plant pests. If you want to keep a ladybug for a little while, you must, right away, provide it with food.

Have a quart container ready. In it put a batch of aphids. How many? About 100 will do for a day or two.

Where do you find aphids? On plants. Favorite ladybug plants include cornflower, centurea, geranium, allium, dill, fennel, marigolds, sunflowers, mint, nasturtiums, roses and weeds. Have an adult help you find and gather aphids still on stems. They won't fly away, but they may drop off the stems.

Bring the container with you. Put a wet tissue in the container so the ladybug has something to sip. Don't put in a water dish, as most ladybugs can't swim.

Now you can find a ladybug. Brush it onto your hand. Be very gentle. Cover it with your other hand, or it will fly away. Then let it go into the container. Soon, if it is daylight, you will be watching the ladybug eat aphids.

Set her, or him, free after a day or two. Ladybugs are not really meant to be pets. If you want to keep the ladybug longer, you must provide about 100 aphids a day. Otherwise the ladybug will starve in your container, and that's not good for the garden or the ladybug. It must fly away home.

Chapter Nine:
<u>IT ALL STARTED WITH A LADYBUG</u>
<u>Iona & Peter Opie</u>

Iona and Peter Opie are authors of many books on superstitions, nursery rhymes and their history, as well as childhood games and fairy tales. How did this all get started? Back in 1944, a ladybug rested on Peter Opie's finger. Without even thinking about it, he started chanting an English ladybug rhyme. His wife, Iona, began wondering where the rhyme came from. A simple enough question, but it started them on their life's work in 1945.

In 1951, their first book, the Oxford Dictionary of Nursery Rhymes, was published. The Opie's referenced and collected toy books, comics, children's magazines, penny dreadfulls, chapbooks, battledores, and over 12,000 hard bound reference books. Other books include Tail Feathers From Mother Goose: the Opie Rhyme book, People in the Playground, My Very First Mother Goose, The Oxford Nursery Rhyme book, Wee Willie Winkie and other Rhymes, The Treasures of Childhood: Books, Toys, and Games from the Opie Collection, and many others. Their reference collection is now found in the Bodleian Library, Oxford It all started with a ladybug.

VOCABULARY

ANTENNAE: The two feelers on top of an insect's head.

APHIDS: Soft, very tiny, insects that feed in groups. They feed by sucking out the juices or sap from leaves and other plant parts.   Aphid feeding weakens plants.

ARCHAEOLOGIST: Person who studies the history of a group of long-ago people by items they have left behind.

DUNG: Waste matter given off, or excreted, from the body.

ELYTRA: Top wings

EXCRETED: Given off from the body, as an insect's waste matter.

GREENFLY: a European name for aphids.

HIBERNATE: To sleep, or stay still through winter.

HONEYDEW: The sugary, sticky, waste matter given off, or excreted, by insects.

INSTAR: The stage in an insect's life between molts, or skin shedding.

INSECTICIDE: A chemical used to kill insects.

LARVAE: The young that hatch from some insects eggs. Larvae do not look like the parents.

MANDIBLES: The jaws or hard parts of an insect's mouthparts

MOLTING: Shedding skin, hair or feathers and replacing them with new growth.

POWDERY MILDEW: Fungi creating a whitish coloration on plants

PREDATOR: An animal that hunts or kills other animals for food.

SCALE INSECTS: Very tiny insects that are usually hidden under a soft or hard covering. Scales feed by sucking out plant juices. Scale feeding can kill plants.

SPECIES: A species name is different for each type of animal or plant

SWARM: very large group

Some Scientific Names for further reference

- Note: When researching ladybug names, you may find them as ladybug, ladybird, or lady beetle. For example: 2 spot ladybird, 2 spot ladybug, 2 spot lady beetle. Also, from time to time, entomologists, or insect specialists, decide a new name is necessary.

-

- 2 spots   2 spot ladybug   Adalia bipunctata

   twice-stabbed ladybug   Chilocoris stigma:

photo credit: Valerie

7 spots 7 spot ladybug or C-7 Coccinella septempunctata

9 spots   9 spot ladybug   Coccinella novemnotata

10 spots   10 spot ladybug   Adalia 10-punctata

Kidney-spot   Chilocorus renipustulatus

11 spots   11 spot ladybug   Coccinella 11-punctata

12 spots   Convergent ladybug   Hippodamia convergens

13 spots   13 spot ladybug   Hippodamia tredecimpunctata

14 spots   14 spot ladybug   Propylea 14-punctata

15 spots   15 spot ladybug   Anatis labiculata

16 spots   6 spot ladybug   Tytthaspis 16-punctata

Orange lady beetle   Halzia 16-guttata

18 spots   Ashy Gray ladybug   Olla abdominalis

22 spots   22 spot ladybug   Phyllobora 22-punctata

24 spots   24 spot ladybug   Subcoccinella 24-punctata

Vedalia ladybug   Rodolia cardinalis

Harlequin, Multicolored or Asian ladybug
Harmonia axyridis.

Red ladybug   Cycloneda munda

Black ladybug   Rhizobias ventralis

Hieroglyphic ladybug   Coccinella hieroglyphica

Parenthesis ladybug   Hippodamia parenthesis

Polished ladybug   Cycloneda munda

Confused Convergent ladybug	Hippodamia glacialis
Water ladybug	Anisosticta 19-punctata
Mealybug Destroyer	Cryptolaemus montrouzieri
Cottony cushion scale	Icerya purchasi
Mexican bean beetle	Epilachna varivestis
Squash beetle	Epilachna borealis

Beetles	Coleoptera
True Bugs	Hemiptera
Dung beetle:	Scarbaeus sacer

HIPPODAMIA?

Several ladybug names begin with Hippodamia. The word comes from the Greek *hippos*=horse and *damazo*=to tame, or "Tamer of horses." What has this to do with ladybugs? A good question, what do you think?

In one Greek myth, Hippodamia was a daughter of King Oenomaus. Pelos wanted to marry her. Her father didn't like the idea. He challenged Pelos to a chariot race. Oenomaus was certain he would win, as he had winged horses. Instead, Pelos and Hippodamia tricked him. Oenomaus was killed. Pelos then married Hippodamia.

In another Greek myth, Hippodamia was the new bride of King Pirithous of the Lapiths people. Centaurs, half man-half horse, were wedding guests. During the wedding, a Centaur tried to kidnap Hippodamia. When this was prevented, he returned with other Centaurs armed with stone slabs and pine tree trunks. A great battle took place. Pirithous, his friend Theseus, plus the Lapiths, fought back and won.

BIBLIOGRAPHY

Adams, Jean, Ed. INSECT POTPOURRI, Sandhill Crane Press, Florida, 1992.

Akimushkin, Igor. ANIMAL TRAVELLERS, Mir Publishers, Moscow, 1973.

Arnett, Dr. Ross H, Jr. and Jacques, Dr. Richard L., Jr. INSECTS, Simon & Schuster, New York, 1981

Berenbaum, May R. BUGS IN THE SYSTEM, Addison-Wesley, New York, 1995.

Berenbaum, May R. NINETY-NINE MORE MAGGOTS, MITES, AND MUNCHERS, University of Illinois Press, Chicago, 1993.

Beverley, Claire & Ponsonby, David. THE ANATOMY OF INSECTS & SPIDERS, Chronicle Books San Francisco, 2003.

Borror, Donald J. FIELD GUIDE TO THE INSECTS OF AMERICA NORTH OF MEXICO, Houghton Mifflin Company, Boston, 1970.

Brewer, E. C., DICTIONARY OF PHRASE & FABLE, Cassell & Co., London, 1970, rp Wordsworth Editions Ltd., Hertfordshire,U.K.

Carpenter, H., and Prichard, Mari. OXFORD COMPANION TO CHILDREN'S LITERATURE, Oxford University Press, New York, 1987.

Cowan, Frank. CURIOUS FACTS IN THE HISTORY OF INSECTS, J.B. Lippincott & Co., Philadelphia, PA., 1865.

De Gubernatis, Angelo De. ZOOLOGICAL MYTHOLOGY, Macmillan & Co., New York, 1872, rp 1978 Arno Press

Evans, Arthur V. and Bellamy, Charles L. AN INORDINATE FONDNESS FOR BEETLES, University of California Press, Berkeley, CA, 1996.

Excell, A.W. THE HISTORY OF THE LADYBUG, Erskine Press, Great Britain, 1991.

Evans, Howard Ensign. LIFE ON A LITTLE-KNOWN PLANET, Dell Publishing, New York, 1968.

Flint, Mary Louise & Dreistadt, Steve H. NATURAL ENEMIES HANDBOOK, University of California Press, Berkeley, 1998.

Hesse-Honegger, Cornelia. HETEROPTERA, Zweitausendeins, Germany, 1998.

Hubbell, Sue. BROADSIDES FROM THE OTHER ORDERS: A Book of Bugs, Random House, New York, 1993.

Kneidel, Sally. PET BUGS, Wiley & Sons, New York, 1994.

Jones, Alison. DICTIONARY OF WORLD FOLKLORE, Larousse, New York, 1996

Kite, L. Patricia. CONTROLLING LAWN & GARDEN INSECTS. Ortho Books, San Francisco, 1987.

Leach, Maria, ed. STANDARD DICTIONARY OF FOLKLORE, MYTHOLOGY AND LEGEND, Funk & Wagnall's, New York, 1972.

McGavin, George C. BUGS OF THE WORLD, Facts on File, New York, 1993

Milne, Lorus and Margery. THE AUDUBON SOCIETY FIELD GUIDE TO NORTH AMERICAN INSECTS AND SPIDERS. Alfred A. Knopf, New York, 1986.

Majerus, Michael and Kearns, Peter. LADYBIRDS, (Naturalists' Handbooks 10) Richmond Publishing Co. Ltd, Great Britain, 1989.

Majerus, Michael. LADYBIRDS, HarperCollins, London, 1994.

Opie, Iona & Peter. THE OXFORD DICTIONARY OF NURSERY RHYMES. Oxford University Press, New York, 1997.

O'Toole, Christopher. ALIEN EMPIRE, Harper Collins, New York,1995. Pickering, David. DICTIONARY OF SUPERSTITIONS, Cassell & Co., London, 1995.

Preston-Mafham, Ken. BUGS AND BEETLES, Chartwell Books, Inc., Edison, N.J. 1997.

Turpin, F. Tom. INSECT APPRECIATION DIGEST, Perdue University, Indiana, 1992.

Waring, Philippa. A DICTIONARY OF OMENS & SUPERSTITIONS, Souvenir Press, London, 1978, rp 1997.

Westcott, Cynthia. THE GARDENER'S BUG BOOK, Doubleday, New York, 1973.

MAGAZINES

Cheshire Wildlife Watch, Great Britain, Winter 2001/2

Fugate, Susan H. and Lee, Sara B., ENTOMOLOGIST CHARLES VALENTINE RILEY'S ARTIFACTS & PAPERS, Agricultural Research, October 2005, pp. 20-21.

Furth, David. BEETLEMANIA! Wings, Summer 1991, p 12.

Hagen, Kenneth S. Ph.D. FOLLOWING THE LADYBUG HOME. National Geographic, April 1970, pp 542-553.

Stephens, Erin J. and Lacy, John E. THE DECLINE OF C-9, NEW YORK'S STATE INSECT. Wings, Fall 2003, pp 8-12.

OTHER SOURCES :   Personal communications
The Xerces Society for Invertebrate Conservation   www.xerces.org

INTERNET

http://www.faculty.ucr.edu/~legneref/biotact/ch-35.htm

http://www.oznet.ksu.edu/dp_entm/dept_news/Riley.htm

http://www.celticbug.com/Legends/Lore.html

http://ohioline.osu.edu/hse-fact/1030.html

http://ohioline.osu.edu/hyg-fact/2000/2002.html

http://www.ojibway.ca/lady.htm

http://www.entomology.umn.edu/ladybird/index.html

http://insects.ummz.lsa.umich.edu/MES/notes/entnotes6.html

http://home.att.net/~larvalbugbio/ladybug.html

http://www.enchantedlearning.com/subjects/insects/Ladybugs.html

http://www.uky.edu/Agriculture/Entomology/entfacts/fldcrops/ef105.htm

http://www.insecta-inspectac.com/beetles/ladybug/

http://creatures.ifas.ufl.edu/beneficial/lady_beetles.htm

PHOTO REFERENCE:

Chris Schuster at www.chris-schuster.com
Stamps: www.asahi-net.or.jp/
Valerie: home.att.het/~larvalbugbio/ladybug.html
Eny3005.ifas.ufl.edu/lab1/Hemiptera/Corixid.html
InsectImages.org www.bugwood.org

ABOUT THE AUTHOR

L. Patricia [Pat] Kite has written 20 children's biological and social science books and authored/co-authored 15 garden books, as well as published over 1000 diverse articles for newspapers, magazines and reference texts. In the process she has earned three Garden Writers of America awards, a National Society of Newspaper Columnists award, a Foliage Writers of America award, and a gold National Parenting Publications Award.

Pat holds a Biology teaching credential among her assorted degrees, and loves to write animal science. She especially loves to write about insects. Like many people, Ladybugs are a favorite insect. The more Pat learned about them, the more enthusiastic she became. Which is how this book came into being.

Besides science, Pat likes stories. Her early years were in Manhattan, P.S. 166. Every week she went to the New York public library for story-telling hour. Today Pat likes stories of "how things came to be," and the myths, lore and legends of insects and plants.

Over the years, Pat has attended Fairfax High School, UCLA, UCMC-SF, UCB, CSUEB, SJSU, and NWCULaw. She lives in Newark, California. Her four children are adults now. They grew up listening to stories too.

L. PATRICIA KITE children's science books,

Bison   (Harcourt Education/Heinemann Library 2006
Sharks (Harcourt Education/Heinemann Library) 2006
Contributor Grzimek Encyclopedia juvenile reference--
Mammals, 2005
Contributor Grzimek Encyclopedia juvenile reference---
Reptiles. 2005
Leeches (Lerner Publications Company) 2004.
Raccoons (Lerner Publications Company) 2003.
Insect Facts and Folklore (Millbrook Press) 2001.
Cockroaches (Lerner Publications Company) 2001.
Dandelion Adventures   (Millbrook Press) 1998.
Silkworms (LPK Science) 1997.
Blood-Feeding Bugs & Beasts   (Millbrook Press) 1997.
Amazing Insects ([Houghton Mifflin) 1996.
Building a Birdhouse (Houghton Mifflin) 1996
Gardening Wizardry for Kids   (Barron's Educational Press)
1995
Insect-Eating Plants (Millbrook Press) 1995
Sea Slugs Down in the Sea   (Albert Whitman & Co) 1994
Crabs Down in the Sea (Albert Whitman & Co) 1994
Octopus Down in the Sea (Alb ert Whitman & Co) 1993
Jellyfish Down in the Sea   (Albert Whitman & Co) 1993
Noah's Ark –Opposing Viewpoints (Greenhaven Press,
Inc.) 1989

TO ORDER

For information on school or library presentations, write to below with self addressed envelope.

To order **Ladybug Fact & Folklore**, enclose check or money order :

   $12.95 & $2 p/h= $14.95

to:

LPK Science
5318 Stirling Ct.
Newark, CA 94560-1352

YOUR NAME:

YOUR ADDRESS

CITY AND STATE

ZIP CODE

ORDERING INFORMATION
<u>Please print</u>

YOUR NAME:

YOUR ADDRESS

CITY AND STATE

ZIP CODE

Check or money order must be enclosed

LPK Science
5318 Stirling Ct.
Newark, CA 94560-1352

$12.95 per book

postage/handling $2. for one or two books